Helping Paws

Service Dogs

by Jane Duden

Perfection Learning®

Cover Photos: ©Haga
Interior Photos: ©Wayne Kryduba: pp. 2, 4, 11–19, 29, 31, 34–36, 40, 44–55.
  ©Anita D. Schermer: pp. 22, 27, 28, 33.
  ©Jen & Pete Peterson-Berridge: pp. 8–10, 23, 24, 26, 30, 32, 42.
  ©Kathi Carlson: p. 39.
  ©Haga: pp. 6, 37.

About the Author

As a freelance writer and former elementary teacher in Minnesota and Germany, Jane Duden has written 28 nonfiction books for children. She writes for teachers and kids on many topics but with great enthusiasm for animals, science, and the environment. Her quest for stories and adventures has taken her to every continent, including Antarctica. At home, she likes cooking, swimming, biking, in-line skating, and learning new things. She enjoys speaking at schools because she likes the spirit and sharing of young authors.

Jane lives in Minneapolis with a houseful of pets.

Acknowledgments

With sincere thanks to the volunteers of Helping Paws of Minnesota, Inc., and especially to Eileen Bohn, Program Director and Helping Paws Co-Founder; Jenny Peterson and Pete Berridge; Deb Johnson; Dorice Russell; Sharon Peters; Jessica Hagenah; Joe Fouks; Julie Trebtoske; Anita Schermer; Dawn Torine-Micko; and Todd Limond.

Dedication

This book is dedicated to an extraordinary golden retriever named Alpha. He began his Helping Paws career at seven weeks of age. Through the experience of his training to be a service dog, the Helping Paws program was created. He was the Alpha: the first, the leader. More than 25 Helping Paws placements later, it was still Alpha who proved it could be done. He enriched Jenny's life and the lives of everyone who met him.

Alpha retired in 1997 after nine years of devoted service to Jenny Peterson.

🐾 Table of Contents 🐾

When You Need a Helping Paw

Imagine being unable to open a door, get the phone, or pick up something you drop. These are problems that people with physical disabilities face each day. Now imagine having a furry, friendly helper who opens the door, gives you the phone, and picks up things. When you need a helping paw, it's always there.

Paw, you say? Yes! The paws belong to dogs that are specially trained as helper dogs. They are called *service dogs* or *assistance dogs*. Night or day, home or away, they are willing and loving helpers.

For people with disabilities, service dogs make possible the things we take for granted. The dogs do many tasks their owners are unable to do. They turn lights on and off. They push elevator buttons, pull wheelchairs, and retrieve things. They open and close drawers and doors, pull off coats and socks, and more. One owner's life was saved because his service dog brought him the telephone so he could dial 911.

Helping Paws is also the name of an organization. Helping Paws of Minnesota, Inc., is a group of volunteers. They raise and train service dogs. Then they place these dogs, free of charge, in the homes of people who have physical disabilities. In this way, Helping Paws helps people with physical disabilities live more independent lives.

A service dog and owner are a special team—the dog lives to serve as a life-long companion and friend. And the owner is able to live life more fully because of these helping paws. Let's meet some Helping Paws dogs and their people!

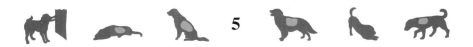

5

Chapter

Special Teams

Jenny and Alpha

Jenny and Alpha were one of the first service-dog teams in Minnesota. Jenny was an athletic, artistic, social 17-year-old when she had a downhill skiing accident. A spinal cord injury left her disabled.

Jenny spent many months healing. Her disability meant she had to use a wheelchair. It meant that she could not do all the things she was used to doing.

Still, Jenny went forward with her life. She started college. She took up archery. She moved into her own apartment. And she got a van.

Jenny had always loved animals. She'd ridden horses and had pets. Now animals were missing from her life.

So four years after her accident, Jenny got Alpha. Eileen Bohn, the co-founder of Helping Paws, was Alpha's trainer. At 1½, Alpha was a light-colored, medium-sized, big-hearted golden retriever. Eileen believed that Alpha could help a disabled person live a more independent life. Along came Jenny.

"When I heard they were starting a service-dog program in Minnesota, I got really excited," said Jenny. "I was in the right place at the right time."

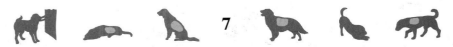

Eileen, Alpha, and Jenny trained together. "Helping Paws taught me what I needed to do for Alpha. So he could work for me," said Jenny. "I learned to think like a dog because Alpha can't think like a person." And Jenny and Alpha began their life as a terrific team.

"The biggest thing when I first got Alpha was the physical tasks he did for me," said Jenny. "But soon it became the contact, companionship, love, and devotion between us. Before I got Alpha, people looked past me. It was hard to deal with. I felt really out of place. And I didn't want to be out in public. Being in a wheelchair is not an issue anymore. And it's mainly due to Alpha.

"Because he was with me, I had the confidence to go out into the world with a different body image," Jenny continued. "I was the same on the inside, but there were things I couldn't do anymore. Alpha didn't care that I couldn't do everything for myself. Alpha's unconditional love and acceptance brought my self-confidence back.

"He gave me a purpose to be out because I had to take him on walks. I went to Lake Calhoun with my dog, just like other people. I belonged."

Alpha went everywhere with Jenny. They visited schools and talked to groups. Jenny explained her disability.

"When I was injured, the neck bones pinched together. This killed the nerves that send the signals from my brain to the rest of my body. You know how lamps must be plugged into electricity to work? Well, it's like the plug was pulled at my neck. The connection was broken. So no signals get to my legs or feet."

But that didn't stop Jenny. She and Alpha went to college. "Alpha was on my lap in my picture for the yearbook. He was at my side when I graduated."

At Jenny's graduation from Augsburg College in 1990, Alpha graduated too. He got a very special ovation from the audience when they went up to get Jenny's diploma. Alpha looked like quite a scholar with his lacy bow tie and serious look.

Jenny works as the Coordinator of Volunteers at Courage Center in Minneapolis. Alpha goes to work with her.

Courage Center helps people with disabilities learn to live the best lives they can. Jenny was a patient there after her accident.

"Alpha's job is to get me up and going each day," Jenny explained. "He's excited to go to work. He opens the door with a pull. He waits for me to wheel out of the house. I say, 'Get the door,' and he pulls the door shut. It's fun to see him jump in the van and be excited about the day."

Alpha likes to work for Jenny. He likes having jobs to do.

He gives the pizza delivery person the check at the door. When Jenny and Alpha go to the grocery store, Jenny puts a basket on her lap. Alpha picks up anything she drops. He likes to do his own shopping too. He picks dog treats off the shelf and carries them to Jenny.

Jenny and Alpha have had many adventures. They have modeled. They went to the Paralympics, where Jenny competed in archery. And when Jenny married Pete, Alpha was in the wedding. He carried the rings in a basket and shook hands with the guests. He sat by Jenny's side as she said her vows.

Alpha has gone on canoe trips with Jenny and Pete. Jenny and Pete even took Alpha to the Minnesota Twins' World Series in 1991 at the Metrodome. Pete said, "The noise was so loud we had to tie Jenny's jacket over his ears. It looked as if he had a toothache!"

Alpha and Jenny did a lot to spread the word about Helping Paws. Thanks to their example, people signed up to be foster parents. Some donated puppies or money. More people with disabilities applied for service dogs. No wonder Alpha was nominated for 1996's Service Animal of the Year.

   10

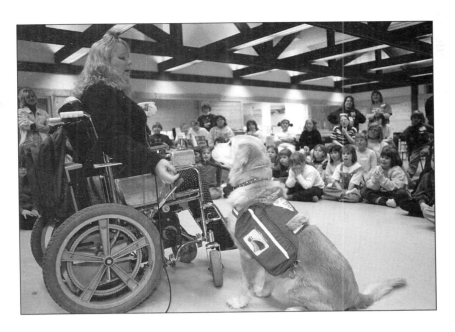

Deb and Barney

Deb and Barney, her Helping Paws golden retriever, visit many schools together. Deb tells kids how Barney helps her in daily life.

Barney went to school to be a helper dog. He started when he was a puppy.

"Barney helps me do things," said Deb. "He is trained to listen to me and follow my voice commands. But he can also understand hand signals."

It was important for Barney to learn hand signals for commands. Then if he ever lost his hearing, he could still be a working dog.

"I can be talking to another person and still give Barney a command," added Deb. "Or if he's too far away to hear me, he can still see the hand signal and know what I want him to do."

"Barney needs to focus on me. I also have to prove Barney is under control. When he is in public, he has to act like a service dog. Not like a pet dog."

Deb talked about Barney's backpack. The backpack is his uniform. When Barney has it on, he knows he has a job to do. The backpack also shows that he is allowed in public places. Like schools, grocery stores, malls, restaurants, theaters, libraries, and medical clinics. Barney can even ride in an airplane or on a bus because Deb needs him by her side.

Barney's backpack says "Dog At Work, Do Not Pet." Deb explained that even though Barney is a very friendly dog and would like to be petted, he would be distracted. Then he might not give her the help she needs.

Deb and Barney showed their audience how they work as a team. She asked a volunteer to put items from her backpack on the floor. Then Deb said with a cheery voice, "Look, Barney! Get it!"

One after another, Barney picked up the items. He picked up keys, a pill bottle, a remote control, and a portable phone. He retrieved a ruler, a dime, a bracelet, a hairbrush, and a book.

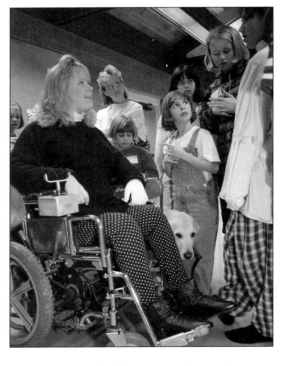

As Barney picked up each item, he carried it to Deb in his mouth. She said, "Give, Barney," and he dropped it in her lap. "Good boy! Good job!" Deb said each time. The students clapped for Barney's good work.

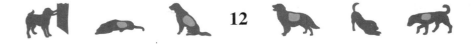

Deb was in a diving accident when she was 16 years old. That's why she's in a wheelchair. She dove into shallow water and broke her neck. This injured her spinal cord.

Deb warned kids never to dive into shallow water. "Your spinal cord carries messages from the brain to the body," Deb explained to her listeners. "An injured spinal cord cannot be repaired.

"There are many types of disabilities," Deb continued. "Millions of people have disabilities. Some are born with their disabilities. Others become disabled through accidents or diseases. Not every disabled person wants or needs a dog. But I do."

Deb is able to move her arms, but she can't move her hands very well. And she can't move her legs by herself.

Deb's van has a wheelchair lift so she can get in and out of it. But someone else needs to drive because Deb doesn't have enough upper-body strength. During the day, she drives her electric-powered wheelchair to get around.

Because of her disability, Deb needs a helper with her always. People come to help her for a few hours every day.

But Deb has always wanted her own dog. "I didn't know if it would be possible because of my disability. I wondered if I'd be able to take care of the dog's needs—feed him, pet him, brush him, nurture him, and also have control over him. And I didn't want the dog to bond to my parents or my boyfriend or my attendant. I wanted him to bond to me.

"I worried about taking the dog everywhere with me," Deb continued. "Sometimes it's hard enough for my wheelchair to fit through a door, in an elevator, or down a crowded aisle. Let alone having a dog connected to me."

But Deb didn't need to worry. Helping Paws volunteers teach both the dogs and their handlers what they need to know.

Deb explained. "All people who get Helping Paws dogs must take a special eight-week dog behavior course. You learn how a dog thinks and learns. You find out that dogs are pack animals. So *you* need to be like the top dog in a pack. Then your dog will listen to you and feel comfortable. When you don't act like the top dog, your dog might feel unsafe or worried.

"Sometimes I go to the Helping Paws Training Center to join a class and practice with Barney. Just like any skill, you have to use it or you lose it. That's why I'm happy that Barney and I do a lot of demonstrations. It gives us lots of practice. I don't want him to forget any commands."

Barney helps Deb feed him. She said, "I keep his food in a cupboard. I tell him, 'Get the door!' He pulls open the door with a pull cord tied to the handle. Next I tell him, 'Get the drawer!' Barney grabs the pull cord and pulls open the drawer." Then Deb gets out a cup and fills his food dish. When Deb says, "OK," Barney eats.

Deb has a big fenced yard where she and Barney play ball. Deb and Barney also enjoy long walks on a paved path around a nearby lake.

"I may not have a lot of strength in my arms," said Deb. "And I can't push my own chair or drive my van. But I have complete control over a 62-pound dog. I'm pretty proud of that!"

Dorice and Hombre

"Easy! Easy, Hombre!"

That's Dorice talking to her service dog, Hombre, when he pulls her wheelchair. She talks loud so people can hear them coming—especially if Hombre's going full speed!

Hombre is a big yellow Labrador retriever. Pulling Dorice in her wheelchair is Hombre's favorite job. Because Dorice had

polio as a baby, she needs to save her muscle strength. She can walk with crutches but usually rides in her electric wheelchair. Sometimes she uses her manual wheelchair.

Dorice wanted a dog to pull her manual chair because it takes so much of her strength. "Hombre pulls me on floors, carpet, sidewalks, and rough terrain. When I need to use my manual wheelchair, I can count on Hombre to pull me. And I know he has the strength to do it," said Dorice.

Hombre also likes going to work with Dorice at JC Penney's. Most customers are thrilled and surprised to see Hombre in the store. He helps Dorice with her job.

Hombre picks up hangers off the floor. Dorice said, "I don't have the abdominal or leg muscle strength to lean over and pick things up. Now Hombre does that for me."

Dorice tells him the commands. "Get it, Hombre! Give! Good boy!" Sometimes Dorice says, "Down, Hombre. Good dog." Then he lies down to watch quietly or doze. Hombre is very good in public. He's quiet and follows Dorice's commands.

Dorice says everyone at work spoils Hombre. Dorice's supervisor, Sharon, keeps treats for the big yellow dog.

Sharon said, "If you're going to put a dog out on the floor where 2,000 shoppers walk through every day, the dog has to be predictable and good with kids. Hombre is well-behaved on the sales floor. And he's wonderful with customers. He knows when he's working. And he knows when he's on break.

"Hombre is interesting to watch," Sharon added. "He stands, listens, and waits for Dorice to come back from the coat locker. It's easy to see how he cares for Dorice."

Hombre and Dorice were teamed when Hombre was only 18 months old. Both of them have lots of energy and love to have fun. "We're a good team," said Dorice. "Our personalities match. He's my loyal friend. He likes to cuddle. When I start stirring or the alarm goes off to wake me, he nudges me and gets on the bed. And he has the most expressive eyebrows. I've never seen a dog's eyebrows work like his. They go up and tilt so I can tell when he's scared, happy, or not thrilled about doing something. It's hilarious!"

Julie and Dakota

"I believe I got the best dog," said Julie when she was asked about her service dog, Dakota. Dakota is a yellow Labrador retriever. He helps Julie by picking up dropped items, pulling her coat and shoes off, and turning light switches on and off.

Julie added, "I feel more secure having Dakota around. He can get the phone if I need it or pull the door open for me."

Julie was born with muscular dystrophy, which makes her muscles weak. She uses an electric wheelchair to get around.

Julie and Dakota attend Augsburg College. Julie will soon graduate as an elementary teacher.

"Dakota goes to class with me," explained Julie. "It works out really well. He lies down and sleeps during class like he's

trained to. We're training him to put books into my backpack.
He's really, really good at retrieving."

Julie continued. "Our relationship is a working relationship.
We're a team." Julie wants people to respect that and not to
interfere. People often
want her to stop and tell
about Dakota. She likes
that, but not when she's in
a hurry!

"Dakota goes with me
most of the time," said
Julie. "I hardly ever leave
him home. But sometimes,
it is good for both of us to
have a break."

Dakota knows he's not going along when Julie tells him,
"I'll be right back." This is very hard on Dakota.

"I ask baby-sitters to stay with him sometimes," said Julie.
"Some environments aren't good for him. A loud concert or a
loud party are examples. People could be careless and step on
him. So sometimes I must leave him home for his own comfort
and safety."

Julie and Dakota have fun together. Dakota's favorite
activity is playing with tennis balls. They like going to her
cabin. "We go boating, take long walks, and have campfires,"
Julie said.

Julie looks forward to having her own classroom and
students. Of course, Dakota will be part of her class too. Julie
knows kids love to help and be a part of things. "They'll be
willing to help and cooperate," she explained. "Almost
everyone remembers a certain teacher who really made a
difference for them. I'm hoping that will be me . . . and
Dakota!"

   17

Joe and Kirby

Someone to pull his wheelchair when he goes to college. Someone to take care of. Someone who needs him. Joe got that someone—a big black Labrador retriever named Kirby.

Joe was born with cerebral palsy. Not all of his muscles do what he tells them to do. So Joe was thrilled to have a service dog.

Joe feels honored to work with Kirby. "What's important for me isn't so much what Kirby can do. It's having someone who's willing to share his life to make mine better. It isn't like I couldn't get through life without him. But what he does for me is wonderful. And he asks for so little in return—just a pat or a thank you. He doesn't ask for anything more than praise and love. He's happy if I throw him a tennis ball or let him roam in the weeds."

Joe continued. "I owe him so much because of what he gives back to me. I owe him the best veterinary care. I owe him the best training that I or someone else can give him. I owe him the right to be treated with respect and dignity. Never to be yelled at, laughed at, pulled this way and that, or hit.

"Some people feel that when you have a service dog, you take away the dog's right to be a dog. But a dog thinks, If you treat me right I'll do anything just to make you happy. And that's what makes this work."

Jessica and Tony

Jessica likes people's reactions to Tony, her Helping Paws black Lab. Once she and Tony were in the grocery store. A small child saw Tony wearing his blue pack and yelled, "Look Mom, it's Super Dog! He's wearing a cape!"

To Jessica, Tony *is* Super Dog. Tony opens doors, gets her wallet out when she needs it, and even opens the refrigerator to get her a can of Coke. Tony can take off Jessica's shoes, socks, gloves, and jacket.

"I was born with muscular dystrophy," explained Jessica. "It's a disease that prevents muscles from developing fully. And they deteriorate quickly, so my muscles are weak."

Jessica talked about her decision to get a dog. "I read something about service dogs a long time ago, when I was in eighth grade. I thought, boy, I'd really like to get a service dog."

So when Jessica graduated from high school, she applied to Helping Paws. It took 2½ years to get Tony.

"I applied for a service dog because I wanted to feel more secure," she explained. "I wanted to be more independent. Before, I didn't feel comfortable going out in public by myself. And I never would have gone to school before I got Tony. I can count on him to do things like push a button to open a door if I

    19

can't." Jessica and Tony attend Minneapolis Community College, where Jessica is majoring in counseling.

Jessica explained the difference Tony has made in her outlook. "They told me in training class that I'd get a lot of attention because of my service dog. They were right. I've been in a wheelchair all my life. Now that I have Tony, people don't notice me at all. They notice Tony. I like it because people are not staring at me anymore. They see Tony and then say, 'Hi! What's your dog's name?' "

There is a downside, as she explained. "There was one thing I had to get used to. Now people want me to listen to all of their dog stories while they're petting Tony. It can be annoying if I'm in a hurry."

Jessica is proud of her service dog. "Tony can learn anything. He's one of the brighter bulbs on the tree. That's why I like him. He doesn't think like a regular dog. He strategizes. He plans things out."

Jessica shared a funny story. "Tony never used to come into the bathroom with me when I took my shower. Then he started putting on a lot of weight. I wondered how he could gain so much. Well, I soon found out. While I was in the shower, he was eating our other dog's food. Then he was going downstairs and eating the cat food. Now he comes into the bathroom with me. We're working on losing the pounds."

Jessica told more about her service dog. "Tony helps me every day. But one time, he *really* helped me.

"I can't turn myself at night. So I have an intercom. When I push it, my mom comes and helps me turn over. One night, Mom didn't turn her intercom on. So she couldn't hear me calling her. It was 3:00 in the morning, and Tony was asleep. And when this dog is asleep, *he's asleep.* I was scared because my mom wasn't answering me. I'm saying, 'Tony, go get help!'

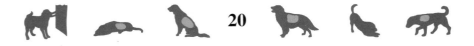

and Tony's snoring. When he finally woke up, he stood outside my mom's door and barked until she got up. My family and attendants know that Tony is finding help when he comes to them barking. And he doesn't stop barking until someone comes."

Tony goes almost everywhere with Jessica. "Tony sits in class with me. He's real good about that. In class, I use hand commands. If he stands up, I signal him to drop. And he'll lie down again. When I have appointments, he goes in, sits down, and waits. He's like a person."

But Jessica doesn't take Tony everywhere. "I don't take Tony anyplace that isn't safe for him. Like a loud place or where the people might be out of control. I don't take him to places where I think he'll be scared.

"For example, when we went to my brother's soccer tournament, a marching band was practicing in the parking lot. The noisy drums freaked Tony out. He tried to climb up in my lap and would not move! So I don't take him to parades."

Jessica is proud of her dog. "Tony is very smart. He clearly understands when I say, 'Pick up the coat. If you don't get the coat, you don't get the treat.' When we put his pack on, he looks kind of sad. But he does take his job seriously."

A notch on Jessica's wheelchair holds Tony's leash. "I can't hold him. He's too big! He's so happy when we're on a walk and we see other dogs. And if he wasn't leashed, he'd chase a squirrel anywhere.

"He lets us know when he wants to play," Jessica explained. "He gets a toy or rope to play tug and brings it to us."

Jessica and Tony like to play ball by a lake. "I throw the ball out for him. He swims out and pushes it even farther! Tony can swim forever. I am so happy to have Tony. He has really changed my life!"

Chapter 2

Training the Dogs

How Does a Dog Become a Helping Paws Dog?

It takes a special animal to become a service dog. Not all dogs are right for the job.

Helping Paws chooses golden retrievers and Labrador retrievers for their service dogs. Goldens and Labs are proven and accepted by the public in service-dog roles. These dogs are large and strong enough to do the jobs of a service dog, such as opening doors and pulling wheelchairs. These breeds have a natural retrieving instinct, which is very important for a service dog. They have soft mouths—good for carrying things. They really like to work. And best of all, they love to please their owners.

   23

It is important to choose service dogs carefully. Eileen Bohn, director of Helping Paws, explained. "By choosing purebreds, we can better predict the weight, size, and instincts the puppy will have when it grows up. We also need to know the background of our dogs to avoid future health problems. A healthy dog means a longer, happier life together for the teams."

Helping Paws also has its own dog-breeding program. In addition, the group relies on puppies donated by purebred dog breeders. People who donate puppies are very special. Helping Paws is honored to be entrusted with these puppies. And what lucky dogs they are to have a special mission in life!

Eileen chooses the puppies when they are seven weeks old. She looks for a puppy with the right personality. Will it be easy to train? Is it dominant or submissive? Does it want to please? Does it love learning?

Basic Equipment

Helping Paws dogs wear royal blue uniforms. For puppies in training, that means royal blue puppy capes. Older pups and dogs wear special harnesses and royal blue packs. The packs identify the dog as a working service dog. The dogs can carry lightweight things like treats, plastic bags, their owner's ID, or an extra leash in their packs.

Dog's work pack

Top of pack

DOG AT WORK DO NOT PET

"Gentle Leader"

A Helping Paws dog wears a special halter collar called a ®Gentle Leader. The ®Gentle Leader fits over the dog's nose. It rests far back on his face. The dog can still open his mouth to eat, drink, pant, retrieve, and bark.

The ®Gentle Leader is like power steering. It enables a person with a disability to keep full control of the dog without using much strength. The collar works somewhat like the halter a horse wears. A dog wearing a ®Gentle Leader will go where he is led.

Thanks to the 1992 Americans with Disabilities Act (ADA), service dogs may go wherever the general public can go. Dogs in training (trainee dogs) also have the same rights. Helping Paws dogs always carry a copy of Minnesota's own state law in their backpack. Sometimes people don't know about the law. So if a store owner or a customer says, "Sorry, no dogs allowed," the law is proof.

Who Trains the Dogs?

Helping Paws service dogs start their training in foster homes. The many foster homes are the backbone of Helping Paws. Volunteers take these puppies into their hearts and homes for about two years. They work with professional Helping Paws dog trainers.

A puppy chosen for the program goes to a foster home between seven and twelve weeks of age. This is the best learning time in a puppy's life. During this time, the puppy is most open to learning and very easy to teach. Putting the pups with other people and dogs at this time is important. It is the right time to start gentle, positive training.

"Foster parents" attend dog-behavior class with their dogs. These classes are held weekly at the Helping Paws Training Center. In addition, the dogs and their foster parents practice lessons at home every day.

Foster families give the puppies comfort, love, and security. They introduce them to crowds, cars, strange buildings, other animals, public places, and much more. They also teach the dogs basic commands. Foster parents record the public places they have taken their dog and the skills they have practiced.

Dogs are assigned to their owners with disabilities once they have mastered service-dog skills. Imagine how hard it is for the foster parents to give up the dogs they have trained! They are sad but also thrilled and proud to see what the dog can do for the happy recipient. Many times, foster families "baby-sit" the dogs they've trained when the dog's new partner goes out of town or on vacation.

Anita and Luther, Foster Parents

Anita and Luther are Dylan's foster parents. Dylan came to live with them when he was seven weeks old. He wore a tiny puppy cape when he started training.

Anita decided a long time ago that she wanted to train a service dog. "It goes hand-in-hand with my interest in dogs and 20 years of working with people with disabilities," she said.

Anita talked about the training process. "When the pups are very young, we help them learn to deal with new people, new places, new noises, new walking surfaces, and things like that. We try to gently guide them into as many different situations as possible. This is important while they're still young and gung ho. It gives us lots of chances for reinforcement.

"One of the first things we teach a dog is a training signal," Anita explained. "The signal is a word that means a treat or praise is coming. We can pick any word we want."

Anita talked about her experience with Dylan. "We chose *whee!* as Dylan's training signal. Then we taught it to Dylan. We sat with him and a dish of his food. We said the word *whee!* and gave Dylan the food. We kept doing this over and over. Soon he started looking for food when he heard the word. He had learned his signal."

Anita continued. "After Dylan knew his training signal, I used it to teach him other commands. When Dylan came to me after I said 'Come,' I said *whee!* and gave him a treat. When I said his name and he turned to look at me, I said *whee!* and gave him a treat. I said 'Get dressed,' and if he looked at his jacket, I said *whee!* and gave him a treat."

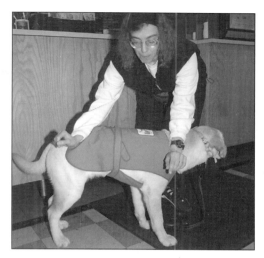

Anita described more training. "When we taught Dylan to sit, we didn't even use the word *sit* until he was already sitting. I held up the treat. Then I guided him into a sitting position. Then I gave the behavior signal *whee!* because he was doing what I wanted him to do. Then I gave him the treat. That's how we teach all the behaviors."

Anita went into the kitchen. Dylan was learning how to open the refrigerator door. "Dylan!" she called. "Get the door! Try again. *Whee!* Good job!"

Pete and Poohbah

As Alpha got older, Pete and Jenny planned for his retirement. They wanted another dog to stay home with Alpha. Pete said, "Alpha hates to be home alone. He scratches at our doors, trying to get out. In fact, he opens the doors and comes running out. That's one of the drawbacks of having a well-trained dog.

"So we started thinking about training a Helping Paws puppy. Then Alpha would have a friend. If the dog made it through the program, he could be placed with Jenny. So we got Poohbah."

Pete talked about Poohbah's progress. "Poohbah is 18 months old. We've been training since she was nine weeks old.

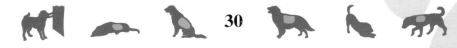

Alpha seemed to say to Poohbah, '*I'm* the people around here and you're just a dog.'

"Alpha has helped me with Poohbah's training," Pete continued. "For example, if I wanted Poohbah to sit and stay, Alpha would hear those commands. So he'd sit and stay. But Poohbah would follow me as I walked away. Well, after a while, Poohbah started looking at Alpha staying there. And before long, Poohbah stayed. So Poohbah picked it up by being the tagalong."

Jenny helped Pete with the training at home. Especially in the things she needed—opening and shutting the doors and picking up things. Poohbah just loved to pick up things for Jenny. If Poohbah saw something drop, she wanted to pick it up right away and hand it back.

Pete explained the importance of a service dog's uniform. "You put the jacket on the dog when you're training. When the dogs are really small, you're always training with the pack on. When you go to class, you always put the pack on. When Poohbah is wearing her pack

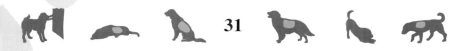

around 18 other dogs in class, she knows she can't be chasing those dogs or barking at them.

"There's a huge difference in how Poohbah acts when she's wearing her pack and when the pack is off," Pete offered. "It surprises people. When people at work asked if they could pet her, I took her pack off first so they could see the difference."

Pete commented on Poohbah's behavior without her pack. "With her pack off, Poohbah went nuts. She ran around from person to person. They were petting her, and she was acting just like a regular dog. Then I said, 'Come on, let's get dressed.' I put her pack on, and she quickly went to my side and sat down again."

Pete talked more about his relationship with Poohbah. "Poohbah goes everywhere with me. At work, she likes the pop machine. She likes the clanking noise when the change comes back. Sometimes a coin will pop out, and Poohbah will pick it up. At the grocery store, she'll take my check and hand it to the cashier. They say, 'Please come back with your dog!'

"Only a few managers have come up to me in stores. 'Sorry, no dogs,' they'll say. I explain, and it's fine. I think it's easier now than when Jenny first got Alpha ten years ago. People are more familiar with service dogs and the laws."

Pete said that most people don't realize how smart dogs are. "I feel like a genius when I work with Poohbah because she learns so fast. But the truth is, dogs are smarter than we give them credit for. It's my duty to find the time to work with her so she can keep learning new things."

Commands

Dawn is a Helping Paws trainer. She teaches foster parents how to train their dogs. She had this to say. "Dogs must understand that their partners will give them the commands they need. A service dog must listen to her handler or partner no matter how strong or weak the command is. Our goal is to train service dogs that will immediately respond to verbal commands."

Dawn described some of the commands.

Around: The dog turns halfway around. This is helpful for grooming and getting uniforms on.

Back: The dog moves backwards. This should work from the front, side, and heel positions.

Behind:	The dog gets in back of you. This is important for halls or aisles, where the dog moves behind you and stays there. This command is also useful in public places such as stores. If the dog gets ahead of you and doesn't know where he's going next, he starts turning around and hitting things with his tail.
Better go now:	The dog relieves himself.
Car:	This means any vehicle—bus, van, or car.
Carry:	The dog carries an object in her mouth while moving with you.
Drop:	The dog lies down.
Easy:	The dog slows down or takes something out of your hand.
Fix it:	The dog untangles his legs from the leash. The dog learns to pick up his feet, and he learns good body awareness.

   34

Get dressed: The dog puts his head or nose into his uniform or ®Gentle Leader.

Get it: The dog retrieves. (Get the ball, get the phone, get your leash, and so on.)

Get the door: The dog pulls on a door pull attached to a handle to open or close a door.

Go get help: The dog searches for someone to come and help.

Hold: The dog holds something in her mouth without chewing. Also means holding a door open.

Kiss: The dog licks your cheek. Putting peanut butter on your cheek can help the dog learn this.

Leave it: The dog ignores or doesn't pick up an object, like food. This command also means not to chase a squirrel!

Let's go: Encourages the dog to come with you, leave a room, or go on a walk.

 35

Light: The dog activates a switch or button with her nose.

My lap: The dog places her front paws on your lap. Use this to get kisses or a hug, groom the dog, or get him dressed. Also works if the dog is retrieving something and bringing it back to you.

Off: Tells the dog to get off an object or a person.

Paw: The dog raises right paw.

Phooey: The dog stops what she's doing.

Put: This is different from give. It tells the dog to drop what's in his mouth. For example, use this to have the dog put your credit card on a store counter.

Right: This means shake, extend, or lift the right paw.

Rise: The dog stands on her hind legs and places her front paws onto a surface.

Snuggle: The dog comes up and places her head on your shoulder.

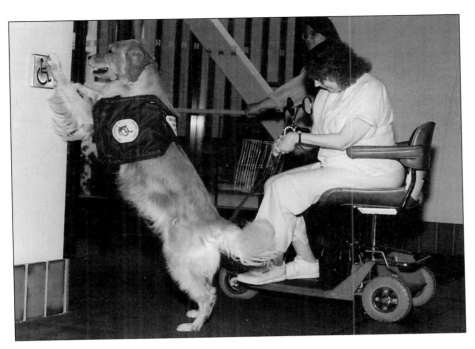

Speak: The dog barks on command. This can be a lifesaver when you need rescuing.

Switch: The dog uses his front feet to activate automatic door openers.

Take it: Say this to the dog when you hand something to him. At a store, the dog can take your credit card from the clerk and bring it to you.

Tug: The dog pulls while moving backwards. Puppies do this for fun. They use it to take off gloves, coats, or socks.

Under: The dog goes under your desk or under a table, as in a restaurant.

Undress: The dog removes his head from the uniform or ®Gentle Leader.

Wait: The dog can move a little but can't cross a barrier. Also means to wait before eating as you put down the food dish.

   37

"Several commands can work together," explained Dawn. *"Go ahead* tells the dog to go through a door before you. Next you might say *around* to get the dog looking at you. Then *back* until you're through the door. Finally, *side* to come back to your side. Use these commands to keep the dog paying attention to you!"

Dawn continued. *"Release* tells the dog he doesn't have to do that command anymore. If the dog is pulling open a door, he needs to pull until you say *release.* If you're on a walk, say *release* to let him off duty. Then he can sniff around for a while. If he is lying someplace to be quiet until you need him, you can say *release* to let him get up. But owners need to be careful when they say *release.* It's not wise to use this command in a restaurant because the dog will probably get up and shake. The fur will fly! It's better to say *come* or *heel* so you can get outside before the dog shakes."

After the dog knows a command, she needs practice with distractions. This is the way it will be in real life.

Dawn dreams up all kinds of distractions for the dog classes. She rolls or bounces tennis balls back and forth. The dogs must not chase them. She makes popcorn and drops it on floor in front of the dogs. Foster parents say *leave it* and correct dogs who go for the food.

Dawn brings in a remote control dog or wind-up animals that zoom around. Once her husband brought his pet pigeon in a harness. This was hard on the retriever dogs! But they must learn to *stay* or *leave it.* Service dogs need to keep their attention on their partners.

What Happens If a Dog Does Not Pass Training?

Sometimes a dog doesn't work out because of health or behavior. It's never a problem finding a home or another job for him. For example, the foster homes might keep him as pet.

Sacha is an example. Some service-dog organizations train standard poodles because they're smart and easy to train. They are good for people who have allergies. So Helping Paws got Sacha, a poodle.

Sacha was smart and quick to learn. But as she went through training, she developed some health problems. This prevented her from being placed. So Dawn kept Sacha as a demonstration dog.

Sacha's new job was to educate people about Helping Paws and what service dogs can do. "She loved to put her pack on and go to work," said Dawn.

Dawn and Sacha traveled all over Minnesota. They visited children in hospitals and senior citizens in nursing homes. Sacha's trademark was her wonderful, gentle kisses.

    39

Chapter 3

Forming Teams

Getting a Helping Paws Dog

Jessica told how she got her Helping Paws dog. "First, Helping Paws came to see if I needed a dog. Next they wanted to know more about me. I answered questions about myself, and so did five of my friends. Helping Paws put it all together to figure out which dog's personality was most like mine. It's important to get a good match.

"Then I went to the training center," continued Jessica. "I worked with some dogs that were almost finished with their training in foster homes. We saw which dog I worked best with. You can tell when a dog will work for you. And sometimes, you might not work well with any of the dogs.

"Tony and three other dogs were in the first group," added Jessica. "Three other people were there, but Tony wouldn't listen to them. He just wanted to be with me. The other dogs were dragging me this way, pulling me that way. I couldn't work with them! But Tony did whatever I asked. I knew right away that it was Tony or none of the dogs out of that group."

Jessica did not leave with a dog. She explained what happened next. "Three months later, Helping Paws called. They

41

said I could have Tony if I still wanted him. They told me about the training classes I needed to attend.

"The eight-week dog behavior course came first," explained Jessica. "After I passed that, I went to team training with my dog. Helping Paws said even after I had Tony, I could choose to say it's not working out and give him back. But it IS working out!"

How Much Does a Helping Paws Dog Cost?

Helping Paws volunteers do all the raising and training of the dogs. The cost of breeding, raising, and training each dog is over $7,000. But the dogs are given to the recipients at no charge. The recipient pays only a $25 application fee and a $100 equipment fee.

What Is Team Training?

After a team is matched up, they go through team training. They must learn how to work together.

This is what it was like for Jessica and Tony. "For three weeks straight, every day but Friday, Tony and I went to class together at the Helping Paws Training Center. Other Helping Paws dogs and their partners were there too. We learned how to talk to our dogs and how to get our dogs to work for us. We learned all the commands. Then we went to public places and learned how to work with our dogs.

"The first day of class was really hard," said Jessica. "The first time I said 'come, Tony,' he stood there looking. His eyes

   42

said NO WAY! So I had to change my voice and get excited. I never expected that. But these dogs do get bored. They need help to get excited.

"The trainers showed us how to call them. I learned that Tony likes little pet names like *Tony Man* or *Mr. T.*"

Jessica continued. "If you and your dog work well together as a team, you get to graduate. But you still have to pass a test to show that your dog is under control."

Testing the Teams

Dogs that go into public places must be stable and well-behaved. Their owners must show that they have control of their dogs at all times. This is why service-dog teams take a test after training together. They take the Assistance Dog International Public Access Certification Test.

The test is usually done at a busy shopping mall. Malls provide many distractions that will test the teams.

Helping Paws volunteers and trainers help Eileen set up the situations. The teams must perform tasks as the trainers watch.

Jessica described what the test was like. "You have to

- show how your dog waits while you unload from the car
- heel your dog through traffic and other dogs to enter the mall
- walk your dog quickly and slowly through store aisles
- show that your dog can back up
- drop the leash and ask your dog to bring it back
- have the dog lie down and have people step over him
- have somebody else take the dog while you go away— to see if the dog gets excited or anxious
- get your dog to walk past food on the floor

- have your dog pick up things you drop
- have your dog stay while you walk away
- sit in a restaurant and show that your dog can be out of the way and quiet

"They also have another dog there to act as a distraction," Jessica added. "This extra pet is one your dog doesn't know.

"The trainers also throw clipboards on the floor behind you while you're walking. This checks whether your dog will get scared or just ignore the noise."

Jessica added a final thought. "And remember, there's always more training if a team needs it."

Chapter

Dogs Will Be Dogs

Joe remembered the first morning after Kirby moved in. "It was the year we got a 36-inch snowfall on Halloween. I said, 'Kirby, Let's go outside!' I was sitting inside with no shoes on. Kirby was outside at the end of his leash.

"The next thing I knew, out ran a white squirrel. Instantly, Kirby thought *Chase! Retrieve!* He started running, pulling my chair until his leash ran out. I went flying into the snowbank. No shoes, no jacket. And I couldn't move because I was stuck in the snow. I did a lot of praying and a lot of yelling. Somebody waiting at a stoplight saw me and went to get help."

Jessica had a story to share. Her family learned not to put anything but soda pop in the downstairs refrigerator if the puller strap was on the handle.

"Tony watched my mom put a cake she made in the 'fridge downstairs. Then he sat down and waited for her to leave. Mom noticed Tony hadn't come upstairs. She headed back downstairs to find out why. And she got there just in time to catch him.

"Tony had pulled the pan out of the refrigerator onto the floor. He was licking the top of the cake. She yelled, 'Tony!' He turned his head as if to say, 'Oh, no.' I thought it was hilarious. Mom thought it was funny too!"

"Barney used to embarrass me horribly when we'd visit schools," said Deb. "If I didn't bring treats, he'd just sit there and pretend he didn't know anything."

Deb laughed. "I take treats with me everywhere we go. And I explain to the kids. 'You know, Barney is not a robot. I can't just expect him to do everything perfectly every time. He has his days.' "

Dorice told about a time when Hombre was stubborn. He wouldn't retrieve. "He would just space out and look everywhere else. So Eileen came and we went to the training center. We worked on retrieving once a week for a few weeks. That helped him and it helped me. I learned to motivate Hombre by using a lively voice or making it a game."

Anita took puppy Dylan to a theater. Their front-row seats were not a good idea. When the actors jumped forward with spears, Dylan barked! Anita quickly moved to a seat farther back.

Even Alpha's not perfect. He has stolen pizza off the counter, scratched all the doors in the house, and thrown up in meetings. Back when Jenny first got him, Alpha loved chasing

squirrels. Jenny would park her van on campus and open the door. If Alpha saw a squirrel, he was out of the van like a rocket.

So Eileen took charge. She went to college with them. Eileen did squirrel training with Alpha. He learned to ignore the squirrels and pay attention to Jenny.

Now Jenny is back at college to earn her master's degree. And she has Poohbah with her. So far, she has eaten two of Jenny's books and some very important notes!

Chapter 5

What's the Best Part?

The owners talked about what they most enjoy about their service dogs.

Deb said, "I get to have my best friend with me everywhere I go. I'll never forget the first time Barney and I were at a class. He lay next to me and put his head right on my feet. It was so touching and so adorable. It was his way of saying, 'I'm here. Just let me know whatever you need.'"

Shannon is teamed with Blaze, a golden retriever.

"Blaze has really changed my life. It's the first time that I've had to be responsible for someone else. He's like having a kid. When we go somewhere, I pack his toys, treats, food, and favorite blanket."

Charlene is teamed with Honey, a golden retriever.

"Honey can pick up boxes and cans from shelves in the store when I am shopping. She puts them in the lower shelf of the cart.

"She is also a good friend and companion. One who's always there to love me. In public, Honey makes it easier for people who may feel uneasy about approaching a person with a disability."

Joe explained, "Kirby always looks to me first. He is willing and eager to do whatever I need."

Jessica said, "Tony's really changed my life. Because I have a disability, I'm always depending on other people to take care of me. But nobody depended on me. Tony changed that. He depends on me. That gives me self-esteem. Tony likes everybody, but he thinks he and I are a pack. So that's a nice thing he's added to my life."

Todd is the foster parent for Daisy Mae, a black Lab. "I like watching her develop and learn week by week. She's just a wonderful companion. She's very, very smart."

Foster mom Anita said, "When Dylan leaves, we will miss him a lot. But when I see what he can learn and do, I know he'll make someone a really good service dog."

Pete said, "Every day I see how Alpha really changes Jenny's life. I don't think people realize what an impact they have on someone's life when they train the dog. It makes the

quality of a person's life so much better. Living with Jenny, I have the opportunity to see this every day."

Now you see that dogs are more than a "human's best friend." To someone with a disability, a service dog can make all the difference in the world!

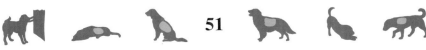

Chapter 6

Saying Farewell

Dogs don't often outlive people. The teams shared their thoughts about saying good-bye.

Joe had these thoughts. "The hardest part is realizing your dog won't be around forever. Kirby is eight years old. He won't be here for as long as I want him to be. I can love another dog as much as I love Kirby. But still, another dog can never replace Kirby."

Big dogs, like Labs and goldens, can be service dogs for as long as ten years. They can live about 15 years. As they get older, they need to rest more. When they aren't able to work, they can retire and become regular pets.

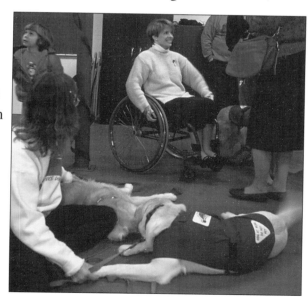

    52

"Helping Paws"

organization whose
to provide service
le with disabilities.

That was the plan for Alpha. He was 11½ when Helping Paws had a festive retirement party for him on February 4, 1997.

Jenny brought scrapbooks with photos. Poohbah came. Other volunteers and their dogs came. Everyone told stories about Alpha and celebrated his great career as a service dog. Alpha was given a certificate and a gold watch on a long chain. Jenny put the beautiful watch around Alpha's neck. But Alpha's health began failing fast. Each day he grew weaker. On February 19, 1997, Alpha died at home. He was surrounded by people who loved him.

Jenny said, "Alpha's death came too soon for all of us. But he will live on in our hearts forever."

Chapter

Meeting People with Disabilities

When you meet someone with a disability, do you wonder what to say or do? These tips from people with disabilities may help.

- Be yourself. Treat me as you would anyone else you meet.

- Respect my right to let you know what kind of help I need. Use good judgment on whether to ask if I need your assistance.

- Talk directly to me—not to the person with me. And if I'm in a wheelchair, try to put yourself at my eye level.

- If I have a speech problem, I may be hard to understand. So ask me to repeat what I say until you understand. Or ask another person to help.

- If I'm deaf and no interpreter is present, talk to me using a normal tone and rhythm of speech. If you speak rapidly, you may want to slow down so that I can read your lips. Consider using a notepad and pencil.

   54

- When my service dog is in a uniform, don't pet him. He's working and cannot play.
- Be considerate and patient with the extra time I might need to do or say things.
- Never start to push my wheelchair without first asking if you may do so. And let me tell you how to push my wheelchair over curbs or stairs.
- Remember that I have many interests. I'm a person like anyone else. I just happen to have a disability.

Index